HALIFAX

DISCOVERING ITS HERITAGE

Stephen Poole

Photography by Keith Vaughan

FORMAC PUBLISHING COMPANY LIMITED
HALIFAX

Formac Publishing Company Limited acknowledges the
support of the Cultural Affairs Section, Nova Scotia
Department of Tourism and Culture. We acknowledge the
financial support of the Government of Canada through the
Book Publishing Industry Development Program (BPIDP)
for our publishing activities. We acknowledge the support of
the Canada Council for the Arts for our publishing program.

All photographs by Keith Vaughan with the following
exceptions: p13 (below) Julian Beveridge; p14 (right) Julian
Beveridge; p50 (above) PANS, (below) United States
National Archives, Washington, D.C., Photo #165-WW-158A-
15AU

Canadian Cataloguing in Publication Data
Poole, Stephen
Halifax, Discovering its Heritage
2nd ed.
Originally published as: *Halifax : a colour guidebook.*
Includes index.
ISBN 0-88780-514-0

1. Halifax (N.S.) — Guidebooks. 2. Historic sites —
Nova Scotia — Guidebooks. 3. Historic buildings —
Nova Scotia — Halifax —Guidebooks. I. Title.

FC2346.18.P66 2000   917.16'225044   C00-950070-7
F1039.5.H17P66 2000

Formac Publishing Company Limited
5502 Atlantic Street
Halifax, Nova Scotia
B3H 1G4

Printed and bound in Canada.

CONTENTS

INTRODUCTION

The Dutch sailing ship Eendracht *in Halifax harbour*

For most of its life, Halifax has been a busy garrison town. Founded in 1749, it was established to counter the military threat posed by the French fortress at Louisbourg, on Île-Royale (Cape Breton Island). Since then the city's fortunes have depended on the military role it played in the evolving relationships of Britain, France, the U.S. and Canada. It continues to depend more than most cities

Military helicopters flying over the harbour; McNabs and Georges islands in the background

on government and the military for its economic prosperity.

Halifax's position in defence has never diminished, although the nature of war has changed drastically. Nevertheless, warships from the various countries in the NATO fleet make regular visits to the harbour, and visiting sailors are not uncommon in the downtown streets. The legacy of being active in two world wars continues, with regular reminders at the cenotaph in the Grand Parade and the Sailors' Monument in Point Pleasant Park. At the same time, as the metropolitan centre for Atlantic Canada, Halifax is a focal point for commerce, higher education and cutting-edge technology. The fisheries are in decline, but offshore natural gas is bringing a new economic boom. The shipyards struggle to find

Sailors' Monument, Point Pleasant Park

Art Gallery of Nova Scotia

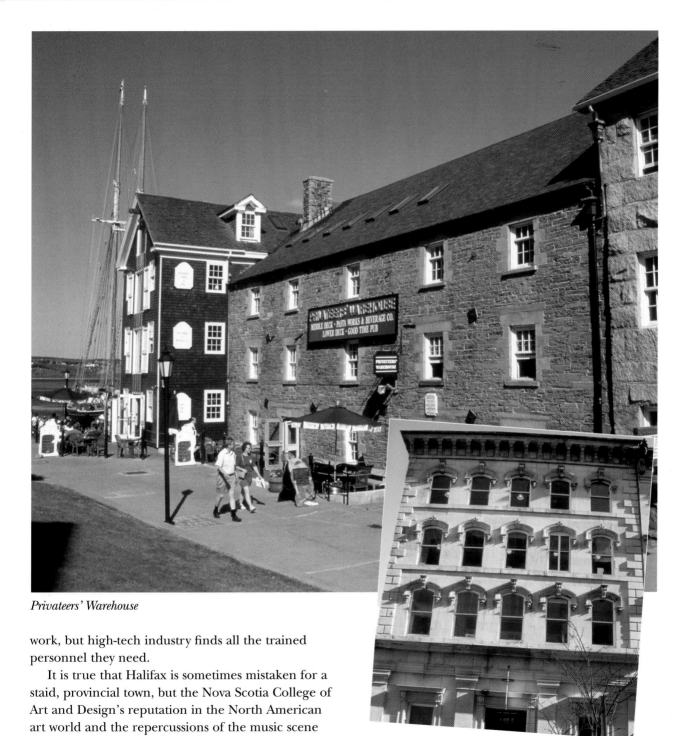

Privateers' Warehouse

Nova Scotia College of Art and Design

work, but high-tech industry finds all the trained personnel they need.

It is true that Halifax is sometimes mistaken for a staid, provincial town, but the Nova Scotia College of Art and Design's reputation in the North American art world and the repercussions of the music scene that has spawned bands like Sloan and artists like

Spring Garden Road, downtown Halifax

Sarah McLachlan, defy those descriptions. It is a vital commercial and government centre with two container terminals and five universities. The provincial legislature resides here, and the city is home to a substantial federal bureaucracy. Many of the more than 300,000 people in the Halifax Regional Municipality work for the government or in government-related service industries.

International Buskers Festival

Crowds watching Tall Ships 2000

So, Halifax looks in many directions simultaneously. Besides the military, one finds Shambhala International, headquarters for a worldwide network of Buddhist meditation centres. Downtown Halifax is a mix of tradition and innovation. There are independent bookstores, coffee shops, gift stores, and galleries tucked in among the office towers and Victorian institutions.

In summer the city seems to spill out onto the streets day and night. There is not a week that goes by without some festival or another, from May until the end of September. These events include the Nova Scotia International Tattoo, a musical extravaganza with a military flavour, the Atlantic Jazz Festival and Dartmouth's Maritime Old Time Fiddling Contest and Jamboree.

A focal point for activity is the waterfront. for Halifax and its harbour are inseparable. The water defines much of the city's existence, past, present and future.

1
THE WATERFRONT

Halifax skyline at night

For many thousands of people, the first touch of terra firma in the New World was the Halifax waterfront, and their first taste of Canadian hospitality was Pier 21. In 1999, a unique exhibition hall was opened in Pier 21 to honour immigrants, especially twentieth-century refugees from Europe. A number of exhibits recall what it was like for new arrivals. Other displays honour the men and women who left from Pier 21 to go overseas in two world wars. Some of the adjacent red brick buildings have been opened up for offices and studios. Here too cruise ships regularly dock so their passengers can visit Halifax.

Towards downtown, along Lower Water Street, the Farmers' Market comes to life every Saturday morning in the Brewery. Growers and other entrepreneurs come from far and wide to sell fresh produce, knick-knacks, ethnic foods, plants, and herbal medicines, while the local residents wander down to enjoy the atmosphere, do their shopping and support local businesses.

Back in 1837, the Scottish-born brewer, Alexander

Pier 21 exhibition hall

Brewery Market, Lower Water Street

Keith Hall on Hollis Street, formerly the offices of Keith's Brewery

Tugboat in harbour

Keith, decided to expand his Lower Water Street premises. With the help of high rum prices (slave labour had been abolished in the West Indies), Keith's business flourished within the imposing ironstone walls of the new brewery. Although the Keith interests were bought out by the Oland family shortly after the First World War, Alexander Keith's India Pale Ale (now brewed by Labatt) remains a favourite beer of Nova Scotians. Today, the restored Brewery is frequently held up as an example of what can be achieved by preservation-minded developers. Its red brick interior, with gothic windows and arches, provides a comfortable setting for restaurants and offices.

Across from the Brewery are the pilot boats that are dispatched to guide large ships in and out of the harbour and the tugs that occasionally tow ships in or out. These floating engines were the inspiration for the popular children's television show "Theodore Tugboat."

Adjacent to this "working" section of the waterfront is the Maritime Museum of the Atlantic, bringing past and present together. Display boards along the waterfront help identify the types of vessels that are moving around the harbour, while seafaring traditions and important maritime events are on exhibit inside. The 1917 Halifax Harbour Explosion and the role that Halifax played in the *Titanic* disaster are given special attention. At the quay behind the museum is *HMCS Sackville*, a Second World War convoy escort corvette, which has been restored as a memorial to those who served in the Canadian Navy. An interpretation centre tells the

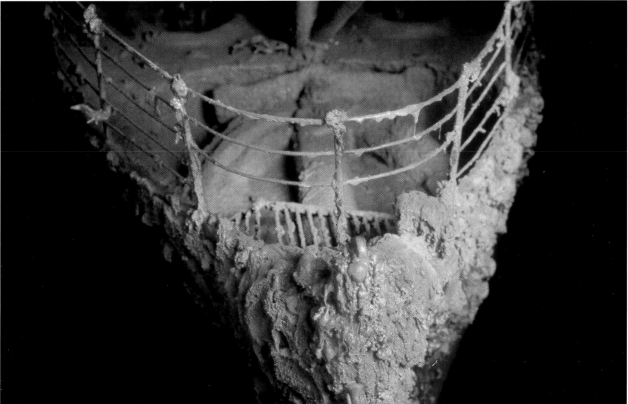

Bow of the Titanic *in its underwater state, covered in rusticles*

HMCS Sackville

story of the Battle of the Atlantic. Also at dockside is the hydrographic vessel *Acadia*, which spent more than five decades surveying waters from the Bay of Fundy to Hudson Bay.

Inside the museum is the old William Robertson & Son ship chandlery, showing some of the gear and devices that still keep wooden boats afloat. In addition, a display of some of the great variety of floating craft, from Mi'kmaq birchbark canoes and a Royal Barge once used by Queen Victoria, to models of passenger liners and working boats, gives a glimpse at maritime history. The museum is also an important place for researchers looking into maritime traditions, shipping and events.

There are many stories to go along with the museum's artifacts. For example, a Swedish greaser aboard the ill-fated *Imo* (one of the two ships involved in the collision that resulted in the Halifax Explosion of 1917) was informed of his own death by the Swedish consul in New York a year later. And a

Ship chandlery store in the Maritime Museum of the Atlantic

Replica of the Titanic

Halifax harbour pilot who was stranded aboard the luxurious *Aquitania* during a storm ended up going all the way to New York. For his troubles, the crew of the *Aquitania* presented him with a tea service, now on display at the museum. A prized artifact in the museum's permanent *Titanic* display is the original record of transmissions from the sinking ship kept by a radio operator at Cape Race, Newfoundland.

During the summer and fall, this part of the waterfront is alive with entertainers and kiosks. Visitors and locals alike spend time just strolling along, looking at the interesting boats that are tied to the wharves, listening to a young musician who is busking for a few dollars, eating lunch and sharing the crusts with the pigeons or ducks.

One feature of living near a harbour is the chance to ride a ferry every day to work. Since 1752 there has been a year-round ferry service from the bottom of George Street across to downtown Dartmouth. Today, there is additional ferry service to and from

Bagpiper on the waterfront

Harbour ferry that runs regular service between Halifax and Dartmouth

Nova Scotia Crystal store

Woodside, another Dartmouth community. The Halifax Ferry Terminal is an architectural feature that makes life for ferry passengers a comfortable form of public transportation. Nearby, in the Nova Scotia Crystal store, experts can be seen turning out fine quality glassware similar to Ireland's famous Waterford crystal.

Redevelopment of the waterfront area began in the 1970s at Historic Properties, just to the north of the ferry terminal. Most old waterfront buildings were slated for demolition to make way for an expressway, but determined citizens halted the road builders as the enormous interchange opposite the Sheraton Hotel was completed. Instead of an expressway, the old buildings (and some later additions) were made into shops and restaurants. The starting point was a collection of ten buildings from Georgian and early Victorian houses and to this was added waterfront warehouses and the stone Morse Building. One building actually withstood a blow from the wrecking ball before the plans for the waterfront expressway were abandoned.

Above the Water Street entrance of the building directly across from Morse's, the word "Bank" is carved into the sandstone. The official name of this bank, established in 1825, was the Halifax Banking Company, but everybody called it Collins Bank. And Enos Collins probably liked it that way. The one-time schooner captain from Liverpool, Nova Scotia, grew to be one of the richest men in British North America. A large part of his fortune came from legalized privateering raids off the New England coast during the War of 1812. His *Liverpool Packet* terrorized merchant shipping. The privateers' booty was stored in

Collins Bank (below); Privateers' Warehouse (right)

a warehouse to the rear of the bank (now "Privateers' Warehouse"). Built in 1813, this is the oldest building of the group. Booty from the U.S. frigate *Chesapeake* was kept here after its capture outside Boston Harbour by the *Shannon* in 1813. (The last words of the *Chesapeake's* captain — "Don't give up the ship!" — remain the motto of the U.S. Navy.) Before the wharf was reconstructed and a seawall built, the wooden buildings nearest the water had loose floorboards that would float freely during very high tides. Some say this allowed small craft to sail under the warehouses at low tide and unload illicit cargoes in the dead of night.

The Old Red Store in the heart of Historic Properties is the home of the Visitor Information Centre run by the Province. Knowledgeable staff can answer almost any question about services for travellers in Nova Scotia and can make arrangements for tours and accommodation. Just outside the centre is a berth sometimes used by the schooner *Bluenose II*. Built in 1963, this is a replica of the *Bluenose*, a working schooner that competed in and won races against American schooners, for which she gained the reputation as the fastest schooner in the world. This replica underwent an extensive refit to make it seaworthy for the G-7 Summit in Halifax in 1995, and it is expected that it will continue its distinguished service as a Nova Scotian ambassador for years to come.

Bluenose II

2

PROVINCIAL CAPITAL

Government House, home of the Lieutenant-Governor

Modern Haligonians have inherited their working capital buildings from a time of conflict between Britain, France and New England. They are present-day reminders of Halifax's eighteenth-century beginnings.

In 1744 France declared war on Britain. In the New World, Massachusetts' governor William Shirley saw this as an opportunity to seize control of the rich Louisbourg fishery from the French. The following year, a group of four thousand New England militiamen, supported by a British naval squadron, attacked the fortress. To everyone's surprise,

Louisbourg fell after a 46-day siege.

During the intense negotiations that followed the end of the war in 1748, the British sacrificed Louisbourg in order to hold on to some of their European gains. In 1749, Louisbourg was returned to the French, but the British had awakened to the strategic importance of Nova Scotia; it could protect New England from any French designs on the territory. In large part, this realization was a response to the angry and fearful New Englanders.

So, the colonization and fortification of Nova Scotia became part of British policy. In June of 1749, Colonel

Edward Cornwallis and over two thousand settlers arrived in the harbour. Although Cornwallis doubted the mettle of the new colonists (most were disbanded soldiers and sailors), he had no doubts about the site chosen for the new colony. He and his officers agreed that the harbour was the finest they had ever seen. The town of Halifax, named after the head of the Board of Trade and Plantations in London, was built on the western shore.

The first winter was especially hard: the settlers were unprepared for the harsh weather and there were numerous deaths due to typhus. As Cornwallis's statue in Victoria Park illustrates (he is portrayed facing east towards London), this was a place that was looking to England for its *modus operandi* to protect British interests on the east coast and up the St. Lawrence River. Although Cornwallis had brought a large group of civilians — as many more arrived in the following years — with the intention of starting settlements of British subjects, his plans went somewhat awry because the settlers were afraid of retaliatory attacks from aboriginals. Cornwallis refused to negotiate with Mi'kmaq leaders.

The majority of permanent new residents at this time in Nova Scotia were French-speaking Roman Catholics, known as Acadians, who were farming the dykelands around the Bay of Fundy. For one hundred or so years they had adjusted to the exchanges of French and English rule, depending on which treaty was in effect, and until their expulsion, beginning in 1755. Port Royal, and later neighbouring Annapolis Royal, were the British administrative centres for the region, which at that time included all of present-day

Statue of Edward Cornwallis, founder of Halifax

New Brunswick, and at times Cape Breton and Prince Edward Island.

Soon after its founding, Halifax became the governor's seat and the centre from which a new Nova Scotia would be built, with British subjects in the Maritimes. In fact, war with France continued as the two empires fought for dominance in the New World. As men and *matériel* poured into Halifax, the town grew into a noisy and disorderly place, which gave rise to a comment that "the business of one-half of the town is to sell rum and the other half to drink it."

Between the end of the Seven Years War and the American Revolution, a time when thousands of New England Loyalists found refuge in Nova Scotia, Halifax stagnated. While Legge, the current governor, was unable to rouse the militia in other parts of the province to help defend Halifax from attack, the merchantmen saw the opportunity to side with Britain. They ensured that Halifax became a base of operation for the navy in the struggle with the colonies to the south.

The arrival of the Loyalists after the American Revolution was a turning point for Halifax. There are no accurate records of the numbers who landed in Nova Scotia, nor of how many stayed or moved on. However, their dissatisfaction with the conditions, both the day-to-day situation and the political and social problems, created tensions and led to a gulf between the "pre-Loyalist" group and the newcomers.

The myth that most of the Loyalists came from the upper strata of society has now been dispelled. The refugees came from all walks of life: one distinctive

The Provincial Court House, Spring Garden Road

characteristic of this style is the symmetry in design, such as the semi-circular wings on either side of the porch. It is assumed that the plans came from a book of house designs by George Richardson, an assistant in the office of the famous English architect, Robert Adam. The main entrance was originally on the harbour side, but this four-storey view is now hidden by a stone wall. The more modest upper side, which used to be the garden entrance, faces the street.

In the same classical tradition, Province House, built on the site of the old governor's residence, is another fine example of Halifax's built heritage. Also constructed of local stone, this is the legislative assembly building. In 1842 it was praised by Charles Dickens as a "gem of Georgian architecture." The Palladian-style building really is beautiful. The plans were drawn up by one of four commissioners, John Merrick, and the work went ahead under the guidance

group were those of African descent who gained freedom from slavery by fighting for the British. Many of these Loyalists were given small land grants in areas around Halifax and Dartmouth.

Among the most distinguished Loyalists to arrive in Halifax were the Wentworths. Sir John was the former governor of New Hampshire and his wife, Frances, stepped out of the shadows to have a life of her own. She had an affair with Prince William Henry, one of George III's licentious sons who spent some time in Halifax.

Nine years after his arrival, Wentworth took over the governorship of Nova Scotia. His vision for the colony far outreached his contemporaries and one of his most memorable legacies was the construction of a new and lavish residence. The cornerstone was laid in September 1800 and it was still unfinished when the Wentworths moved in in 1803. It was eventually completed by his successor in 1807 and the costs far outstripped the funds appropriated for the project.

Government House, as it is called, is a fine example of the Georgian architecture that is seen in eighteenth-century country houses in England. One

Province House, the seat of provincial government

The Legislature

of architect-builder Richard Scott. It took eight years to complete.

The symmetry and regularity of the floor plans, the elevation and the interior design project stability and stateliness — just what one wants in a government. In earlier times when there was an upper and lower house, the Red Chamber was the home to the Legislative Council. The Red Chamber is now used for public functions, showing off its original ornate plasterwork under the abundance of natural light from the tall windows on three sides. It also houses an oak table that came from the *Beaufort*, the ship that brought Cornwallis to Halifax in 1749.

The Legislative Library, between the two chambers, was formerly the courtroom where Joseph Howe made his triumphant speech that helped establish freedom for the press. The hanging staircases and three-sided balcony were added when the room was converted to a library in 1862. So were the eight alcoves—complete with intricate wrought-iron mayflowers (Nova Scotia's provincial flower).

The Nova Scotia Legislature has met in the Assembly Chamber ever since 1819. Dickens remarked that watching the action was like looking at the House of Commons at Westminster through the wrong end of a telescope. Certainly the partisanship would have been familiar to him. Even the portraits of two prominent statesmen, Charles Tupper (a Conservative)

and William Fielding (a Liberal), switched sides of the Assembly Chamber following a change of government!

Of course, there is a wealth of lore within the walls of Province House, including the story of the headless eagles over the door of the South Committee Room. Apparently with anti-American sentiment running high during the Fenian scare of the 1840s, one Member took it upon himself to whack the heads off the accursed eagles with his cane. It is not known whether he ever discovered that the eagles were really falcons.

These two buildings were the beginning of a wave of construction projects that characterize old Halifax. Opposite Province House, on Hollis Street, is a beautiful Italianate structure built to provide offices in Halifax for the new Canadian government, complete with a twelve-foot statue of Britannia seated atop the building. This is now the Art Gallery of Nova Scotia

Legislative Library in Province House

Art Gallery of Nova Scotia, Hollis Street

and houses an extensive collection of Canadian, British and European works. A special gallery is dedicated to the work of folk artists, especially the colourful work of Digby County's Maude Lewis.

Also in the same area is the Nova Scotia College of Art and Design, which occupies several of the old buildings around the Granville parade. The college was started by Anna Leonowens, whose years as governess to the King of Siam's children have been made to last in films, musicals and books. She came to Halifax to join her daughter and son-in-law and was very involved in the town's social life. The college was originally the Victoria School of Art and was on Argyle Street. Now the college is world renowned in fine art, craft and art education.

Another provincial organization that supports the arts is the Nova Scotia Centre for Craft and Design. In addition to running workshops and courses, the Mary E. Black Gallery has a wide variety of interesting exhibits throughout the year. For example, a weaving exhibit may be followed by a display of handmade musical instruments or architectural models.

Halifax's role as the centre of commerce and politics in the province and in the region continues to increase. Some fine commercial structures from the late nineteenth and early twentieth century can be seen among very run-of-the-mill late twentieth century highrises.

Mary E. Black painting at the Nova Scotia Centre for Craft and Design

The Bank of Nova Scotia

3

THE CITADEL

Today's Citadel is the outcome of many rebuildings. What was once the focal point of the town's fortifications is now a busy spot used for a variety of recreational and sight-seeing activities, transforming Citadel Hill from being the centre of military strategy to the centre of tourism in the city.

Since Halifax was founded, the town is reputed to have gathered riches in times of war, and borne the brunt of economic depression during peacetime. Almost from the beginning, there has been a fortress atop Citadel Hill to watch over the town's fortunes. Edward Cornwallis, the first governor of the new colony, recognized the strategic importance of the drumlin that dominated the designated town site and

Town Clock

built a stockaded fort on the hill. A second fortification was built about twenty-five years later, during the American Revolution, to stave off the invasion that never came. Prince Edward, Duke of Kent, greatly expanded the Citadel during his tenure as commander of the garrison in the 1790s. In order to do this, he levelled off the top of the hill. The fourth fortress was the work of the Duke of Wellington, fresh from his victory over Napoleon at Waterloo in 1815. The Americans had shown their true colours during the War of 1812 and with the enemy so close at hand the Iron Duke felt it necessary to protect Halifax's naval dockyard from a land attack. Ironically, the initial plans for the new fortress were drawn up by Colonel James Arnold, son of

Aerial view of the Citadel

Benedict Arnold.

The construction of the fortress under Wellington was a major local industry for more than thirty years. Whether the effort was necessary is open to debate. No attack came. The Citadel's smoothbore cannon were never shot in defence. And, shortly after its completion in 1856, the introduction of long-range, rifled naval guns downgraded the fortress' strategic importance.

Nevertheless, the Citadel has been put to various uses in the recent past. During the First World War, prisoners from the German merchant marine were kept there. Several escaped using kitchen knives, coat-hangers, and blankets—proof positive that, at the very least, the Citadel walls could be breached from the inside out. One prisoner named Bronstein

Smoothbore cannon

Soldiers' living quarters

spent several weeks there in 1917 while officials checked out some suspicious travel documents. The Russian government secured his release and Bronstein, who was, in fact, Leon Trotsky, went on to his place in history.

For much of the Second World War, the Citadel served as temporary barracks for troops going overseas. However, for a few years the Citadel languished, until it was declared a National Historic Site in 1951. Today, it is a major tourist attraction,

Barracks building

where reconstructed fortifications and Parks Canada staff come together, bringing one of Canada's most significant defence works back to life.

The fort's military routines are now carried out as they were in 1869-71. Men and women wearing authentic uniforms take on the roles of soldiers from the 78th Highlanders and the Royal Artillery, along with the roles of sailors of the Naval Brigade. They drill according to instructions laid out in 1860s manuals. There are piping demonstrations. One of the most popular activities is the firing of the noon gun, which can be heard daily throughout downtown Halifax. Alongside re-enactments, visitors can also enter the barrel-vaulted casemates that once housed the troops, as well as the musket galleries and ravelins which were designed to cause trepidation among the attackers.

The signal flags on the Citadel are the last remnant of a visual telegraph system designed by Prince Edward when he was commander of the troops. It was hoped that a series of signalling stations could be used to send and receive messages as far

South Ravelin

Re-enactment of military routines (above); artifacts and displays (below)

away as Quebec. On one occasion, when the prince was in Annapolis Royal, he ordered a flogging to be performed in the Citadel.

Other features that the Citadel offers today can be found in the Cavalier Building where there are exhibits on communications, the four Citadels, the garrison, the ordinance, and the engineering and construction of the fourth Citadel. "The Tides of History," a 40-minute audio-visual presentation, provides a dramatic look at Halifax's military history and the Army Museum has an extensive collection of guns and military dress.

The fortifications around Halifax Harbour were

constructed in different time periods. Some date back to the years when Prince Edward was commander-in-chief, others to the First World War. Many of them can be seen from the top of Citadel Hill, including George's Island, McNabs Island, where there is a fort, Point Pleasant Park, where there are two forts and a Martello Tower, Connaught Battery in Purcells Cove, where there is now a big microwave installation, and York Redoubt, towards the mouth of the harbour.

Preserving the view from the Citadel has been an issue that Haligonians have battled over as high-rise office towers have risen like great concrete sentinels, separating the fort from the harbour it was designed to protect. The slices of viewplane that have survived still provide a splendid vista of the downtown streets

The Town Clock

Inside the ditch

Looking out of the main gate of the Citadel

Drills in the South Parade

towards Dartmouth and towards the harbour mouth.

From around the inland arc of the Citadel there is a view of the Common. It was originally about three times its present size and was used both for animal grazing and for military purposes. Now, much of the land has been taken up with hospitals, schools, the community college, and the Nova Scotia Museum of Natural History. The Common has had many uses including horse-racing, fairs and is still the site of large-scale public events. It was here that the Pope held mass in 1984, and for a few years on a weekend, the roads through and around the Common were transformed into a Grand Prix racing track for a few days. Much of the remaining land is now given over to sports, such as softball, soccer, football, and even cricket.

Citadel Hill has also taken on the role as a venue for public events. The steep sides provide gradient seating for large-scale music concerts, with a stage on the Wanderers' Grounds. It can be the choice spot to watch fireworks on July 1, and in winter, there are few better tobogganing slopes. And on a windy day, kite-flying pre-empts other activities.

Signal masts

4

PRINCE EDWARD'S ROUND BUILDINGS

St. George's Anglican Church, Brunswick Street

Of all the British royalty that have spent time in Halifax, there is one figure who has left an indelible legacy. Prince Edward, as well as being a strong military leader, proved to have a special appreciation for architecture. Today the structures that he built are enjoyed along with the blend of history and legend that accompany them.

Two of King George III's sons made temporary

Prince of Wales Tower, Point Pleasant Park

homes in Halifax in its early years. Prince William Henry, the third son, had such a reputation for dissolute living that his father virtually banished him from England, allowing him to make mischief in the colonies in between bouts at sea.

The fourth son, Edward, was by nature quite different. He was known to be temperate, courteous and hard working, and he was anxious to prove himself to the king as a worthy son. He assumed command of the garrison at Halifax in 1794 and immediately set to work strengthening the town's fortifications. He expanded the fortress atop Citadel Hill, built Martello towers and established Royal Artillery Park to the south of Citadel Hill. Edward was an enthusiastic soldier: military pageantry and parades with regimental bands were frequent and social life around the garrison was part of his style. Yet he also had the reputation of bringing a hard and unforgiving style to military discipline.

There are two other reasons why Prince Edward's sojourn in Halifax lives on in memory: his predilection for circular structures, and his long-term companion. Both are embodied in a small architectural curiosity on the shores of the Bedford Basin. The Music Room, visible from the highway, is one of several circular buildings that the Prince sponsored and it is the only remaining building from the country estate where he lived with his female companion, Madame Julie de St. Laurent.

It is certainly not unusual for royal romances to be out of step with society's norms. While his brother was breaking hearts in ports around the world,

The Music Room, Bedford Highway

Edward was content to take to his various posts his companion, Thérèse-Bernadine Mongenet, the daughter of a penniless French nobleman. They had met in 1790 when Edward was stationed in Gibraltar and came to "an arrangement." She joined him in Halifax and at some point took on the name Madame St. Laurent. This beautiful, kind-hearted woman, who lived with the prince as his wife for more than 25 years, accompanied him to social functions, except when disapproving prudes had a say in the matter, as was the case with one member of the Halifax elite. They lived on the estate that Governor John Wentworth owned. It is now a park called Hemlock Ravine. The houses have all gone, with the exception of the Music Room, a round, ornamental garden temple. Legend has it that the paths that once meandered through the estate spelled out Madame St. Laurent's name.

On the construction side, the Prince did more than merely fortify the town. He helped refine it architecturally. On Brunswick Street he built St. George's Round Church to accommodate the overflow from the "Little Dutch Church" also on Brunswick Street. His interest in this project stemmed

The Town Clock

publications and videos. The clock itself was late: it did not arrive until 1803, after the Prince's departure.

Prince Edward also introduced the Martello towers to North America. Impressed by accounts of a round defence tower on Cape Mortella, in Corsica that had withstood a pounding by two British warships in 1794, he decided to build one here and name it in honour of his brother, the Prince of Wales. In Halifax, other Martello towers soon followed— one, further out the harbour at York Redoubt, and another at Fort Clarence (now the site of the Mauger's Beach Lighthouse, on McNab's Island).

The prince was eventually called back to England, and being the fourth son, he never became monarch. He was, however, father of Queen Victoria, and he left his legacy in other ways. In Halifax he is remembered through stories and structures.

St. George's Anglican Church

from sharing German roots with the congregation, and it gave the town a strikingly graceful example of the round temple form. This design is usually executed in stone in Europe and the Middle East, but St. George's is built almost entirely of wood. In 1994 tragedy brought the church and congregation into the national limelight when fire almost completely destroyed the wooden structure. Fortunately both government and private donations, combined with the faith and fortitude of the St. George's community, helped rebuild both the interior and the exterior of this beautiful building.

The Prince's reputation for demanding absolute punctuality combined with a fascination for mechanical instruments produced the round clock tower on the lower slope of Citadel Hill, a feature that has been used many times to signify Halifax in

5

VICTORIAN HALIFAX

Public Gardens

During the second half of the nineteenth century, Halifax was a flourishing seaport whose wealthy merchant class, many of them immigrants from the British Isles, gave the city its character. Not only was it a time when institutions such as the Halifax Club were built, but it also was a period when schools, hospitals and the courthouse were established. Evidence of the Victorian era can be seen

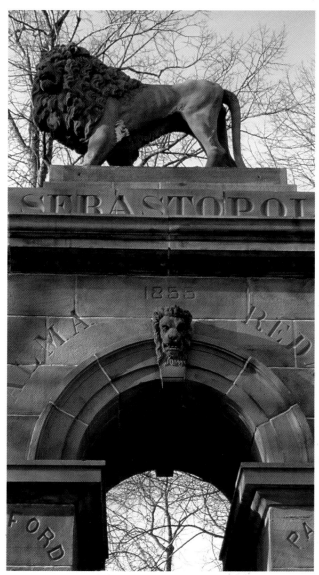

Sebastopol Monument at the Old Burying Ground

groundwork for the state of social welfare in Halifax today, where there are many old and new institutions that help less fortunate people.

Many buildings of Victorian Halifax survive, although their purposes have sometimes changed with the times. Among those that endure are St. Matthew's Church and the Provincial Court House, separated by the Old Burying Ground. They were built within the same decade by a Toronto firm and sport neo-Gothic doors and imposing stone entrances. Above the entrance to the Provincial

all over Halifax.

While the middle class prospered, they did not ignore the less fortunate in their midst. Women's voluntary organizations, such as the District Visiting Society of St. Matthew's Church, helped promote education and welfare and provided fellowship. The work begun by such groups and societies, laid the

St. Matthew's United Church, Barrington Street

Court House there are charming gargoyle replicas, similar to those found on Gothic buildings throughout the British Isles and continental Europe. Both of these edifices reflect the values in justice and religion that were of great importance to the immigrants flocking to Canada.

Unlike the court and the churches the one establishment that was slow in coming to Halifax was a library. The main building, across the street from the courthouse, was not opened until 1949. Previously there had been a small library in City Hall in the Grand Parade.

Before the building boom on Spring Garden Road, which also included St. Mary's Roman Catholic Basilica and the red brick building that is now the School of Architecture for DalTech, the Government House garden covered all of this area.

Now Spring Garden Road is central to downtown activity. It is the premier shopping street, with Mills Brothers, now more than seventy years in business, as

Grand Parade and City Hall

Statue of Sir Winston Churchill in front of Spring Garden Road Memorial Library

the leading establishment for upscale fashions. Although glass and steel have made inroads into the streetscape, the older buildings, like Mills, keep the scale to a more human level. Restaurants, bookstores, coffee shops, gift stores and pubs, as well as beauty salons and other health-related businesses, can be found on Spring Garden Road and the side streets.

The renovation of old residences on nearby Birmingham and Brenton streets is typical of the way that the new and the old co-exist and preserve the flavour of Victorian gentility in the city.

The Lord Nelson Hotel at the corner of Spring Garden Road and South Park Street was grounded on this genteel past in name and in interior decor, although it was opened in 1928. At seven storeys with all of the modern conveniences, it was both an innovation to the city and a defender of tradition, and

Spring Garden Road

Public Gardens

with recent renovations, continues to straddle past and present.

The Halifax Public Gardens is a cherished landmark. It was started by a group of prominent Haligonians who wanted a place to indulge their passion for the "cultivation of choice fruit trees, vegetables, rare plants and flowers." Naturally, the Nova Scotia Horticultural Society, as they called themselves, chose a site along fashionable Spring Garden Road. The gardens quickly became an aesthetic success and a financial burden, with only slight relief coming from the cultivation and sale of rhubarb by the society. Government assistance came, but with strings attached: the society was to make its garden public on a part-time basis.

The city took over the gardens in 1874 and combined it with an adjoining civic garden that had been started a few years earlier. Superintendent

Richard Power, who had gardened for the Duke of Devonshire in Ireland, devised a plan that remains remarkably intact. Pathways, shaded by beautiful weeping trees, meander past floating beds of spring daffodils or summer fuchsia. Subtropical plantings and unusual trees from around the world lend an exotic atmosphere that typified formal Victorian gardens. Griffin's Pond is a remnant of the days when the Freshwater River flowed through the town, making its way to Pleasant Street (now the south end of Barrington Street) and to the "Kissing Bridge," before spilling into the harbour. The river and the bridge are gone, but the Gardens are still in full bloom. At the centre of it all stands the gazebo built to commemorate the Golden Jubilee of Queen Victoria in 1887. Concerts are held here on summer Sunday afternoons. On Saturdays, brides, grooms and attendants can be seen posing for photographers. Not only has Power's plan been very enduring, but some of his descendants cared for the gardens until the 1960s.

Many other city buildings, including City Hall in the Grand Parade, once the site of Dalhousie College, hearken back to the Victorian era—to the time when fortunes were made and Canada was struggling towards federation. The institutions that were established then do more than survive today; they play an active role in Halifax's life and character.

6

THE NORTHWEST ARM

View of the Northwest Arm

The Northwest Arm and the South End are Halifax's affluent communities. They boast grand estates and beautiful parks that wealthy Haligonians began building more than a century ago.

Today these areas grace Halifax with public monuments, trails and leisure clubs, as well as breathtaking private homes.

Finding a view over water that would nourish the

soul and relax the mind has always been an easy thing to do in Nova Scotia. Nineteenth-century Haligonians did not have to go far to find substitutes for the places that the Romantics, such as Wordsworth and Coleridge, were extolling. They merely turned their backs on the town and the harbour and headed for the other side of the peninsula. There they found a sheltered inlet, now known as the Northwest Arm. Bordered by forested hills that nestled tidy coves, it was a perfect place to live the country life, and within one hundred and fifty years of the founding of Halifax, it was lined with estates, boat houses and recreational clubs.

The wealthy elite, many of whom made fortunes in trade with the West Indies, took more and more to the style of landed gentry, building large homes with manicured gardens amid groves of imported trees. For example, Oaklands (about forty acres) and the

George Wright's residence, 989 Young Avenue.

Thorndean on Inglis Street

Belmont Estate (more than ninety acres) were the result of assembling parcels of land which had been granted to settlers in the 1750s. Now, the estates have shrunk and the land has been subdivided into streets of generous houses. A drive through the area and a boat ride on the Arm confirms Halifax's reputation as a place of relaxed gentility.

Closer to the city centre, there are many gracious houses that speak of former fortunes. The examples of variety in architectural expressions, almost all in wood, are too numerous to list. A sample, however, can be found in three homes at the southwest corner of South Park and Morris streets built in the Queen Anne Revival style, a popular choice of wealthy Haligonians toward the end of the nineteenth century. The triangular pediments atop the arched Palladian windows are characteristic of this style. A more lavish Queen Anne style residence at 989 Young was built in

1903 for Halifax businessman (and *Titanic* victim) George Wright. James C. Dumaresq was a busy Halifax architect in those days and many examples of his work, including this one, make the streets of South End Halifax an interesting glimpse at architectural styles adapted for wood construction. Dumaresq also designed many of the commercial buildings in the city.

Many of the houses in the area have associated stories. For example, Thorndean House, built in 1834, is a handsome Georgian home in the Classic Revival style that has a colourful past. In 1838, it was bought by James Forman, one of several prominent Halifax businessmen who had successfully petitioned the House of Assembly for the incorporation of the Bank of Nova Scotia in 1832. Forman became chief cashier (general manager) of the new bank. An esteemed Haligonian, he suddenly fell from grace in 1870 when a junior clerk discovered that Forman had defrauded the bank of more than $300,000 during his lengthy term as cashier. With his career and health in ruins, Forman slunk off to London, where he died a short time later. It seems his ghost lingered in Halifax for a while; a furtive, top-hatted figure had been seen emanating from an old well in the kitchen basement of Thorndean. The well has since been filled in!

A tour of the South End will inevitably lead to Point Pleasant, the extremity of the peninsula. A South Carolina loyalist, Colonel Fanning, built a stone house and cleared land at the site late in the eighteenth

century. Now the whole area is a park, complete with abandoned fortifications. In 1866, on the eve of Confederation, the British Government agreed to lease the 186 acres of wooded parkland to Halifax for 999 years at the nominal sum of one shilling per year (about ten cents). The shilling ceremony still takes place each summer at the park.

Chain Rock Battery overlooking the Northwest Arm, was another important link in the town's seaward defenses. From here, a chain boom once stretched across the water to defend against enemy warships. Close by, the Sailors' Monument commemorates those who lost their lives at sea in two world wars. Further along, Point Pleasant Battery (established in 1762), together with Ives Battery on McNabs Island, guarded the entrance to Halifax Harbour for nearly two

Point Pleasant Park

Sailors' Monument, engraved with more than 3000 names

centuries. During the First World War, mines were laid between Point Pleasant and McNabs, leaving a narrow channel lit by searchlights. Later, a steel anti-submarine net was added. Both batteries stood at the ready.

Fort Ogilvie, Cambridge Battery and Point Pleasant Battery, also in the park, were part of the extensive network of fortifications around the harbour to defend the colony from French attack. They are now overrun with vegetation and make a great place for a scramble with dogs and children, followed by a picnic.

Armdale Yacht Club

A seasonal theatre troupe, called Shakespeare-by-the-Sea, makes good use every summer of Fort Ogilvie and Cambridge Battery for open-air presentations of the Bard's most popular dramas. They have also used the Martello tower, Prince of Wales Tower (a National Historic Site), for the setting of *Hamlet*.

The eastern end of the peninsula offers spectacular views of the harbour approaches and McNabs Island. On fair summer days, this is a good place to watch the bright splash of spinnakers as the boats from two local yacht clubs, the Royal Nova Scotia Yacht Squadron and the Armdale Yacht Club, make for open waters.

Boating is an enduring leisure activity for Haligonians. Rowers, paddlers and small sailboats filled the Arm before the arrival of large yachts. The first organized club, the Northwest Arm Rowing Club, opened in 1899, and within a decade there were two more, each one boasting membership in the hundreds. The one remaining club, St. Mary's Boat Club, has a competitive rowing programme, as well as recreational boating, which offers canoe rentals and sailing lessons.

Several ferries used to run between communities on the mainland side of the Arm, including one from Purcells Cove to Point Pleasant and one from Jollimore, at the present site of Fleming Park. It is almost forgotten that this park, also known as the Dingle, was donated to the city by philanthropist Sir

Sandford Fleming for the express purpose of building a tower that would venerate responsible government in Nova Scotia. This was the first colony in the British Empire to have an elected assembly. The proposed tower was to be in sections of different materials in order to show the evolution of government institutions, the lowest being rough stone, the middle of brick and the top an ornate representation of a sophisticated democracy. The cornerstone was laid in 1908 and the tower was finished in 1912. Today two lions, replicas of those in Trafalgar Square in London, sit at the top of the steps that lead to the base of the tower. This landmark is evident from all around the Arm and the South End of the peninsula, although its origins are somewhat obscure and barely remembered.

There are many of these landmarks, parks and other sites to be enjoyed in the Northwest Arm and the South End. Each has its own history, including some lesser known stories, and most have witnessed well over one hundred years of life in Halifax.

The Dingle Tower

7

THE NORTH END

Hydrostone Market on Young Street

The North End of Halifax has derived much of its character from its economic status within the city. In addition, it felt the brunt of the Halifax Harbour Explosion.

It is difficult to define the boundaries of the North End of Halifax. Does it begin north of North Street or the Citadel? On the east is the harbour, but how far west does the city spread before the North End becomes the West End? Until the 1960s, at its northern limits was the long-established African-Canadian community of Africville.

Although Haligonians use the designations loosely, sometimes with pride, sometimes with disdain, there is a clear distinction between the socio-economic character of the North End and that of the South End. This is evident in the size of the houses, the condition of the schools, the width of the streets, and the types of parks.

This social divide stems from the history of land use on the peninsula. The area around the original town was either military property or, on the west side, part of the Common and therefore unavailable for residential or commercial use. With the development of industry in the late nineteenth century,

Anchor shaft of the Mont Blanc *at Regatta Point Park*

result, the population density of the North End was concentrated in a manner typical of working-class neighbourhoods in cities all over North America—small houses and narrow streets and extended family households.

The North End today, however, is quite different from its origins. The turning point occurred with the disastrous explosion caused by the collision of two ships in Halifax Harbour on December 6, 1917. The devastation was akin to a war zone with whole neighbourhoods destroyed in the blink of an eye. Hundreds of people were killed immediately and many thousands more were injured, blinded by flying glass, buried under buildings, or

factories were drawn to the area north of downtown, near both the railway and the harbourfront. In addition to manufacturing and wholesale businesses, as well as many small businesses related to the fishery and shipping, a large cotton factory was opened on Robie Street in 1883. Today, the remnant is evidenced in the chimney of Pierceys, a building supplies retailer.

The changing pattern of work associated with factory employment meant that housing had to be developed for the workers and their families. As a

physically thrown by the blast. Countless others were swept into the harbour by the tidal wave caused by the explosion.

The disaster occurred at 9:05 a.m. Two vessels, the inbound *Mont Blanc*, a French munitions ship, and the outbound Norwegian vessel, the *Imo*, were attempting to pass one another in the Narrows when the collision occurred. Both ships had pilots aboard, but heavy traffic and a confused flurry of signals brought the two ships together. The *Mont Blanc* was a floating bomb,

1917 Explosion

carrying thousands of pounds of explosives, and after the collision benzol on its deck caught fire. People on shore, in the North End, began to watch the fire. Although there was time for the crew to give due warning about the cargo, they chose to save themselves, knowing that a huge explosion would result if the fire was not contained. The shock wave was heard for miles all around Halifax. Many people, even those who still had roofs over their heads, assumed that there had been an attack by Germans, and in the midst of the devastation that resulted were afraid to stay in the city. In the days that followed, a fierce snowstorm added greatly to the misery of the homeless and to the burden of relief workers, many who were military personnel stationed in Halifax. Any public buildings that were safe were turned into hospitals, morgues and shelters. Help arrived from all over the province, then gradually from other places in the region and notably from Boston.

The rebuilding of the North End did not return the area to what it had been. Large enterprises, such as the sugar refinery, did not rebuild. Not only were small and medium-sized locally-based businesses in ruins, but the families that owned and ran them were shattered by death and injury. Reconstructing houses was only a part of the recovery.

One survivor, fourteen-year-old Barbara Orr, was carried from close to the harbour to the top of Fort Needham by the blast. She suffered an injury to her leg. All of her family died in the blast. As a memorial to them, she donated a carillon of bells to the United

Methodist Church in 1920. Sixty-five years later the bells were removed, with her approval, and placed in the Halifax Explosion Memorial Bell Tower on the fort, now called Needham Park. This hill overlooks the area that was destroyed by the explosion.

To the west, the Hydrostone area at the foot of the hill, is so named for the concrete block that was used for the construction of these houses. The design for the area and for the houses was transplanted from Britain, using the garden suburb model that was being implemented in several large cities. The houses face each other across a common green, and back on to a lane, with small plots behind and at the front of each house. Unlike any of the wooden design adaptations elsewhere in the city, the Hydrostone was a unique

Hydrostone Market

Halifax Explosion Memorial Bell Tower, Needham Park

Africville Homes in the 1950s

and while the houses now sell for premium prices, they were not always so highly regarded.

Another area that was hit very hard by the explosion was Africville. It was a self-contained community on the shores of Bedford Basin, like many of the villages that had grown up around the shore. Being very close to the Narrows, there was much loss of life in this neighbourhood. The first train to come into Halifax after the explosion stopped in Africville, unable to proceed further into town.

Africville was more, however, than a cluster of houses and a church on the outskirts of Halifax. It came to be a place that represents what it has meant to be Black in Nova Scotia. Isolated from the mainstream and deliberately ignored in the rounds of infrastructure improvements—paved roads, water mains and sewage—Africville came to be viewed negatively by city administrators and eventually became a problem for them that had to be solved.

addition to the new North End. As part of the relief effort, the houses were erected very quickly and provided an instant neighbourhood. For the former residents of the North End, this was much different from what they had lost,

Africville reunion

Frustrated at not being able to get city services, some people left the community. Bureaucrats pushed for relocation of the residents and for expropriation and destruction of the properties. Proposals from Africville residents that the area be upgraded starting with the provision of adequate city services were disregarded. Pressure tactics were used by city officials to persuade residents to sell their properties and move.

In the years between the dissolution of the community, and the coming to adulthood of the generation of children who were relocated, the spirit of Africville was born. The Africville Genealogy Society became the focal point for organizing an exhibit, a reunion and a struggle to ensure that discrimination of this nature does not occur again in Nova Scotia.

8

CHURCHES

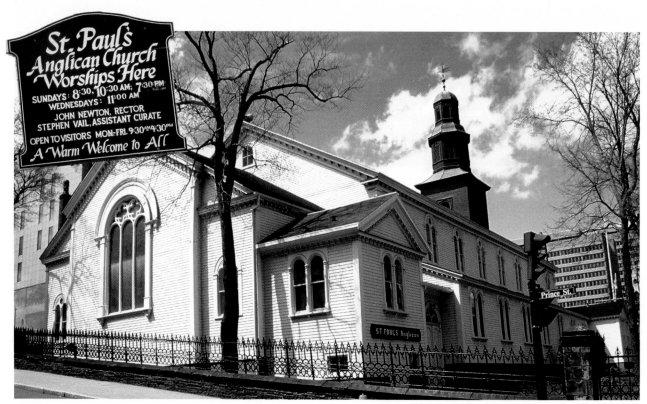

St. Paul's Anglican Church

Although the Church of England was the only official faith in Halifax for years, there has always been wide a variety of religious practices in the city. More and more faiths have taken root in Halifax, as evidenced by the great number of religious buildings to be found. Among the oldest Christian churches in eastern North America is St. Paul's in the Grand Parade. This is the grand dame of Halifax churches. Completed in 1750, one year after the founding of Halifax, it was the first formal religious institution established by the Crown. Seated at the centre of the city, it has retained its original stature as a

St. Paul's Anglican Church

cornerstone of Halifax.

Both the interior and exterior of St. Paul's have been considerably altered from their original states. Like other buildings in colonial towns around the world, the church was patterned on an existing design, in this case James Gibbs' Marybone Chapel in London (now St. Peter's on Vere Street). The unadorned classical features and baroque steeple are typical of the design; however, the expansion of the chancel at the south end, and the additional wings on either side of the nave and the porch at the north end, have transformed the original contours. Galleries added later and stained glass windows give it Victorian touches, but the rough-hewn box pews, reminiscent of a New England meeting house, recall the time when the Church of England shared St. Paul's with its dissenting brethren who had no church of their own in Halifax's early years.

Sermons preached in Mi'kmaq and German were common in the church's youth. It has been said that the history of Halifax is written on the walls of St. Paul's. While not quite accurate, there are many interesting plaques that memorialize men and women who were members of the city's elite. Beneath the floor of the church are the burial vaults of bishops, governors and generals.

Most burials in the early years were in the Old Burying Ground on the outskirts of the town. Now the cemetery is well within the downtown area and is a National Historic Site.

Although Halifax was under the control of the British government, and therefore officially supported only a Church of England minister and church, there were a number of Protestant Dissenters and Roman Catholics among the settlers. Governor Edward Cornwallis was aware that their spiritual needs necessitated the establishment of other churches and meeting houses. Unlike other communities, the deeply etched grooves of sectarianism have been partially

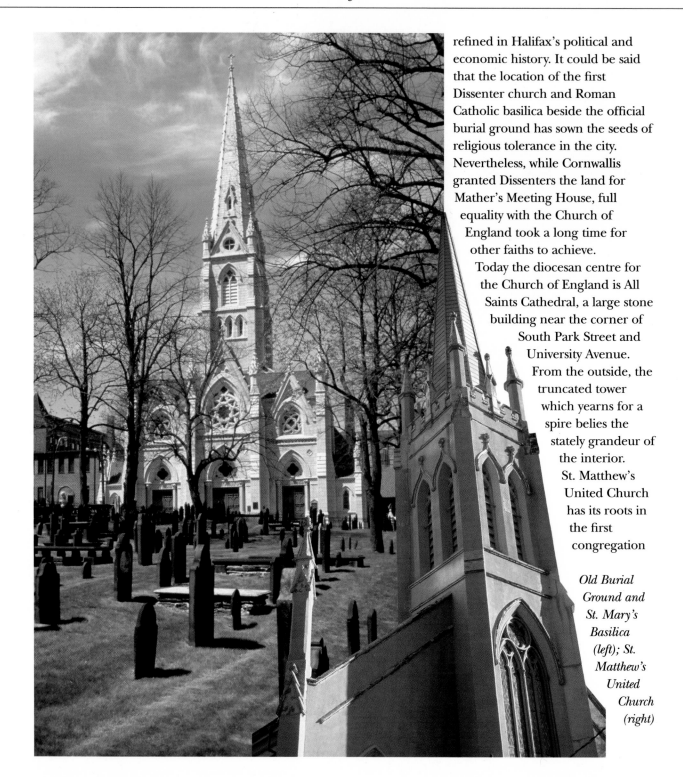

refined in Halifax's political and economic history. It could be said that the location of the first Dissenter church and Roman Catholic basilica beside the official burial ground has sown the seeds of religious tolerance in the city. Nevertheless, while Cornwallis granted Dissenters the land for Mather's Meeting House, full equality with the Church of England took a long time for other faiths to achieve.

Today the diocesan centre for the Church of England is All Saints Cathedral, a large stone building near the corner of South Park Street and University Avenue. From the outside, the truncated tower which yearns for a spire belies the stately grandeur of the interior. St. Matthew's United Church has its roots in the first congregation

Old Burial Ground and St. Mary's Basilica (left); St. Matthew's United Church (right)

All Saints Cathedral

of Dissenters, who were from either the Congregational Church or the Presbyterian Church of Scotland. Later, Methodists, who shared the same Calvinist heritage, would join and eventually St. Matthew's came under the presbytery of the United Church of Canada.

At the corner of Spring Garden Road and Barrington Street is a cluster of church buildings, all part of the Roman Catholic diocese, including the large ironstone structure of St. Mary's which was built in the 1820s to accommodate a growing congregation. The town's original Roman Catholic Church, St. Peter's, was close to bursting its wooden seams by the time the cornerstone of the new church was laid. St. Peter's was eventually dismantled and floated across the harbour, where it rose again to serve as Dartmouth's first Roman Catholic church. St. Mary's was under the spiritual and architectural direction of the first bishop of Nova Scotia, Edmund Burke.

St. Mary's Basilica

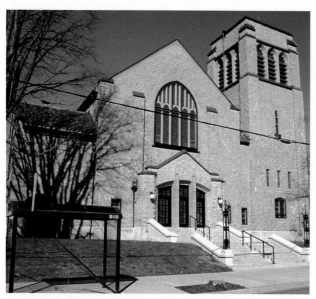
St. Andrew's United Church

During the 1860s, the elaborate Victorian facade and the soaring 189-foot high spire were added.

As the city's residential areas have grown away from the downtown core, so the churches have sprung up to serve the local congregations. First Baptist Church on Oxford Street is one of the well-appointed churches in the South End. It has large assembly rooms and is known for its music, being the site of regular concerts.

St. Andrew's United Church at the corner of Robie Street and Coburg Road is another popular venue for concerts, and features the St. Cecilia Concert series every year. It is also a large stone structure with ample room both in the church and in adjoining buildings.

On Brunswick Street a rare example of Carpenter Gothic style can be found in St. Patrick's Church. The wooden pillars, for example, are painted to resemble marble.

Many churches that have not been declared of

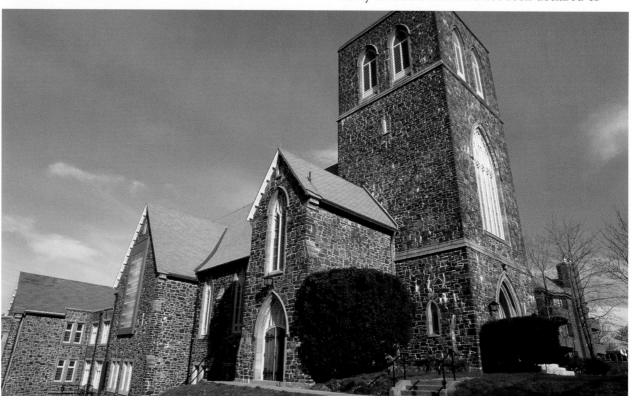
First Baptist Church

historic value and that do not have a wealthy congregation find it difficult to keep coming up with funds to repair, renovate or even rebuild. In the post-war period, there was one remarkable congregant who devoted a great deal of time to building churches. B. D. Stevens was a Halifax contractor who was convinced that communities needed churches. He gave time, money and expertise to help erect many, many churches throughout the Atlantic region. In addition to renovating West End Baptist on Quinpool Road, he built St. Philip's Anglican at the corner of Connaught Avenue and Bayers Road and the Mulgrave Park Church in the North End. Although it was not his intent to become known for his churches, it was his example in helping people that can never be forgotten.

Since the 1960s there has been increasing interest in Buddhism throughout North America, and Halifax is no exception. When the leader of a Tibetan Buddhist group, Chogyam Trungpa, visited Nova Scotia twenty years ago he selected it as a suitable place to relocate his headquarters. Now the Shambhala Training Centre and the Vajradhatu can be found on Tower Road, offering meditation practice and entry into the Buddhist religion.

St. Philip's Church

While Christianity is still the most prominent religion, especially in terms of buildings, the recognition of festivals, Jewish synagogues, a Hindu temple, and mosques are now part of Halifax's multicultural fabric.

West End United Baptist Church

Mulgrave Park Church

9

THE HARBOUR

Tall Ship Rose *in Halifax Harbour*

Halifax Harbour has been used as a port and fishing grounds for centuries. It has also been used in wars. Now, city life crowds around the waterway that was recently surrounded only by nature.

Huge cruise ships, small recreational boats and container ships share the harbour with ferries, naval vessels and various traditional ocean-going craft, as well as with the wildlife on land, in the air, and in the sea.

The Harbour

Extending inland about sixteen kilometers (ten miles) from its seaward approaches, this is the second largest natural harbour in the world. Like much of Nova Scotia's Atlantic coast, the harbour was formed by glacial erosion and the rise in sea level caused by meltwater at the end of the last ice age. Now, the harbour remains ice-free, except for the occasional short-lived episode during abnormally hard winters.

The harbour and the sea beyond affect every aspect of city life. The water does this in obvious ways: its shipping lanes are essential to commerce; it moderates the city's climate, freshening the warmest summer days with sea breezes and taking the edge off winter cold snaps; and it is a source of recreation and pleasure for Haligonians and visitors alike.

The harbour also lends more subtle flavours to life along its shores. In downtown businesses it often takes several promotions to get an office with a harbour view. Together with Citadel Hill, the harbour serves as a reference point for everything else in the city.

Centuries before the Europeans arrived, the Mi'kmaq spent summers along the shores of

Sailboats in Northwest Arm

Chebuktook, "the biggest harbour." For a few short months, warm weather and an abundance of shorebirds and fish made this a most hospitable place.

Tour boats

Deep-sea fishing at the harbour's mouth

Then, the Mi'kmaq would paddle and portage their way across the mainland to return to their winter camps along the more sheltered Bay of Fundy.

European fishermen made similar use of the harbour. It was a convenient port of call during the fishing season. In 1698, the French established a fishing station in Chebuktook on what is now McNabs Island, but permanent settlement awaited a bold British move in their eighteenth-century chess match with the French.

The advantage of the harbour was size, but its importance was enhanced by being ice-free year-round. For communities that have grown up around the harbour, this was and still is a fishing ground, in a limited capacity. Lobster traps are still set off at the mouth of the Northwest Arm, and around Point Pleasant, Purcells Cove and Fergusons Cove.

The close proximity of wildlife and city life is obvious from almost any place around the harbour. It

is an ecosystem that changes and survives amidst the comings and goings of giant oil rigs, submarines, and super tankers. Unfortunately, beneath the surface Halifax Harbour is sheltering from view two and a half centuries of unchecked waste disposal—sewage and garbage of all descriptions. The debate is on, and has been for some time, regarding whether it can ever be cleaned up, with some arguing that disturbing it would be an unnatural disaster. It is some comfort then to see seals basking on the rocks along the shore. In winter, many interesting ducks make this their home, including some northern visitors with very striking plumage. Cormorants and osprey are often seen in the harbour, in addition to the ubiquitous gulls. McNabs Island, in particular, is a favourite haunt of osprey. In spring and summer minke whales make regular visits to the harbour. When word gets out that one has been

seen, intrepid kayakers go paddling to the area.

One of the great boons of modern engineering is that structures can be built above the landscape

Sailing near the Dartmouth shore

Canadian naval vessels

Cruise ship docked in Halifax Harbour

allowing us to marvel at its beauty. Crossing the harbour by bridge, especially the Mackay Bridge, gives a breathtaking view of the harbour and all the activity of port life. The breadth and mystery of the ocean beyond and, in the other direction, the great pool of Bedford Basin are a photographers' delight.

On the Dartmouth side of the Mackay Bridge is the Bedford Institute of Oceanography, a world-class institution funded by the Canadian government. Research carried out here is vital to Canada's position as a maritime nation. Whether it be the study of sharks, tides, icebergs, or underwater geology, the institute plays an important part in ocean research that helps the fisheries, the coast guard, and the broader understanding of marine ecosystems.

Shipping has changed drastically in the last two hundred years. Every few years Halifax (along with other east coast ports) has a taste of the old days when tall ships—large, sail-powered vessels—make a dramatic entry up the harbour. The rest of the year, harbour watchers can see the comings and goings of the Canadian Navy — frigates, submarines and destroyers — and the traffic going to the container ports next to Point Pleasant and Fairview Cove. These great behemoths slide into the harbour, so large that they overwhelm the landscape. More graceful, but nevertheless surprisingly oversized, are the new cruise ships that tour the east coast from June to October. These floating hotels are frequent visitors to the Halifax waterfront, bringing people from all over the world to enjoy a few hours on land.

All of the smaller communities around Halifax Harbour have their particular ways of interacting with the ocean. In picturesque Herring Cove, and in Eastern Passage fishing boats are still part of the landscape, side-by-side with suburban development. In Bedford, the most inland harbour community, the yacht club is a popular place to meet friends before going out for a sail.

Halifax and its harbour are inseparable in the mind's eye. The harbour has been utilized in countless ways, but regardless, it is always a prominent feature of the city.

Tall ship in port

Theodore Tugboat

10
HISTORIC DARTMOUTH

Macdonald Bridge

Dartmouth and Halifax were long-time sister cities connected by the harbour that divides them. For equally long, Dartmouth has had its own identity, beginning with its settlers, and known today for its small downtown, many historic buildings and an abundance of lakes. Now that Halifax and Dartmouth (along with other communities) have been amalgamated into a large municipality, they are more connected than ever, yet still retain their distinctive personalities.

Dartmouth was founded a year after Halifax, when 353 settlers arrived from southwestern England aboard the *Alderney*. Long before this the site was occupied seasonally by the Mi'kmaq who canoed and portaged across the mainland each spring after wintering along the shores of the Bay of Fundy. Relations between the settlers and the Mi'kmaq were hostile because Governor Cornwallis refused to negotiate or consult with the aboriginal people over the new settlement. It is not certain what provoked a violent raid on a sawmill in Dartmouth that left a number of white settlers dead, but records show that life in Dartmouth was especially perilous for immigrants until a 1752 treaty brought peace. The Mi'kmaq view of these events is unfortunately not on record.

From the beginning, Halifax and Dartmouth have been joined at the harbour. John Connor began operating a ferry service in 1752, charging three cents for the hour-long rowboat trip to the opposite shore. The ferry—powered in turn by wind, steam, and diesel fuel—has been running ever since. During the past 50 years ties between the sister cities were further strengthened with the construction of two bridges, the

Alderney Gate

Dartmouth skyline

Broken propeller, damaged by ice

ferry that puts people face-to-face with the salt water and wind, and brings the harbour to life.

Approaching Dartmouth from the harbour reveals at least part of the contrast between the sister cities. The absence of high-rise office towers is an indication that most of Dartmouth's business community is elsewhere, namely in Burnside Business Park. The downtown commercial district takes up just a few buildings around the ferry terminal, including Alderney Gate, which houses a theatre, offices and a branch of the Halifax Regional Library.

The harbourfront walkway, running from Ferry Terminal Park past the Dartmouth Marine Slips to the end of the Shubenacadie Canal, connects many of the sites in this area and gives a view of the Halifax skyline. There is also a broken propeller from the Canadian Coast Guard vessel *John A. Macdonald*, which escorted the SS *Manhattan* on her historic 1969 crossing through the Northwest Passage; the propeller was sheared off by ice.

There are a number of older homes, in the area surrounding the downtown, that give Dartmouth its

Angus L. Macdonald (completed in 1955) and the A. Murray MacKay (1970). They channel the ebb and flow of commuter traffic across the harbour. While the bridges also afford some spectacular views, it is the

Macdonald Bridge

uniqueness among the communities around Halifax Harbour. On Ochterloney Street, there is a fine example of a house with five-sided dormers in the gable roof, a popular innovation that came across the Atlantic with Scottish stonemasons.

Also on Ochterloney is Grace United Church, one of many buildings in the area to rise from the ashes of the Halifax Explosion. Thankfully, all was not lost in the devastation: notably the Quaker house at 57-59 Ochterloney remained. Built in 1786, this is Dartmouth's oldest surviving house and a relic from one of the most interesting chapters of the city's history. William Ray, a cooper who lived in the salt box house at 59 Ochterloney, held the esteemed position of inspector of whale oil at Dartmouth. Today, his house has been partially restored by the Dartmouth

Museum Society. Guides in period costume tell the Quaker whaler's story.

Following the American Revolution, Britain slapped high tariffs on goods from the United States. Among those who suffered, was a group of Quaker whalers from Nantucket who had been supplying the English with sperm oil for street lamps, medicines, and

Grace United Church

Quaker House

cosmetics (they also met the considerable demand for whalebone corsets). In 1785, twenty-four families moved their whaling enterprise to Dartmouth, attracted by a Nova Scotia government subsidy on housing and a colony that was still very British. Their industry flourished along the Dartmouth waterfront until 1791, when the British government pressured them to relocate to Milford Haven, Wales.

Just up the street is the Masonic Hall, built for the Eastern Star Lodge in 1909. Its classical, two-storey pilasters and impressive keystone arch atop the central window befit the Freemasons' devotion to the ideals of construction. In the same area is Dartmouth's oldest church, Christ Church, built in 1817.

Residential areas in Dartmouth have grown up around the network of lakes, which offer recreation during winter and summer, and an ever-changing view over water. International calibre rowers, paddlers and canoeists strain at their oars and paddles on Lake Banook, which has played host to many regattas. This connects with Lake Micmac, and via the Shubenacadie Canal, to Lake Charles. The canal was considered finished in 1861, after more than thirty years of construction. It was built to link the rich farms along the Bay of Fundy with the port of Halifax, following the Mi'kmaq canoe route. Shortly after its completion, the Intercolonial Railway made it obsolete, but the canal workings remain a source of fascination. The canal's interpretive centre in Shubie Park, between Lake Micmac and Lake Charles, preserves this chapter of Nova Scotia's history, complete with a working model of the locks.

Dartmouth is also the birthplace of Nova Scotia's premier folklorist, Helen Creighton (1899-1989). She began her travels by selling medical supplies from a Red Cross ambulance during the 1920s, and quickly

Evergreen, home of folklorist Helen Creighton

developed an interest in the stories and folk songs that she heard in kitchens throughout rural Nova Scotia. She began collecting songs, some of them variants of familiar tunes heard in many parts of the British Isles. Others were more obscure and even original. In time her interest became her profession and eventually, for her contribution to preserving cultural traditions, she received the Order of Canada.

Arrangements of the songs she recorded and had transcribed are used by choirs and folk singers far and wide. One of the most enduring songs is called "Nova Scotia Song," remembered for the chorus line, "Farewell to Nova Scotia, the sea-bound coast." Her collections of folk stories, *Bluenose Ghosts* and *Bluenose Magic* were perennial best-sellers for decades. Her former home, Evergreen House, built in 1867, now houses the Dartmouth Heritage Museum's collection of Victorian furniture. Every year a festival is held in Helen Creighton's name in the Halifax-Dartmouth area.

Until the amalgamation of the communities into the Halifax Regional Municipality, Dartmouth had its own mayor and administration, school board and library. However, despite all the fears of being obliterated by amalgamation, Dartmouth is still very much its own place and the ferry is still called the

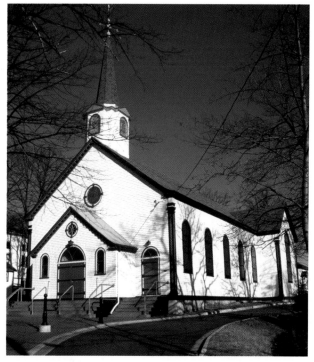

Christ Church

Dartmouth ferry, the library, still the Dartmouth Library and no one would dream of saying they live in the part of Halifax called Dartmouth!

INDEX